PARTY LEGEND

PARTY LEGEND

Sam Duckor-Jones

Victoria University of Wellington Press

VICTORIA UNIVERSITY OF
WELLINGTON
TE HERENGA WAKA

Victoria University of Wellington Press
PO Box 600 Wellington
New Zealand
vup.wgtn.ac.nz

A catalogue record is available at the National Library of New Zealand.
ISBN 9781776564231

Acknowledgements
Some of these poems have previously appeared in other publications,
including *The Spinoff, Sport* and *Verb Wellington*. 'Party Legend' was
commissioned by Melbourne Jewish Book Week 2020; 'Boy Oh Boy
Oh Boy Oh Boy' appeared as exhibition text at Bowen Galleries in
2019; 'O Man' was first published in *More Favourable Waters: Aotearoa
Poets Respond to Dante's Purgatory*, edited by Marco Sonzogni
and Timothy Smith (The Cuba Press, 2021); and '*HI!*' appeared as
exhibition text at Aratoi Museum of Art and History, 2020. Thank you
to the editors and curators.

Published with the support of a grant from

ARTS COUNCIL OF NEW ZEALAND TOI AOTEAROA

Printed in Singapore by Markono Print Media Pte Ltd

Formica – kitsch queen, my rock
& Foresight – thanks for sometimes being there

Contents

*If you shoot an arrow and it goes real high
hooray for you*

—Dorian Corey

Party Legend

Vote for me   I'm from a very distinguished flame /
I attended a school for gifted merchandise /
Yet this is also an everyman's story /
I have a very relatable familiar regular story /

Sure I upended a pool of lifted merchandise /
& I appear to you now as a velveteen seal pup with enormous
bloody teeth, but don't be frightened /
I have a very relatable familiar regular story /
Plus I understand complex economic systems /

I may appear to you now as a velveteen seal pup w an
enormous bank account, but don't be fooled /
I'm from a tiny Kansas farm atop the Himalayas in the
Mexican state of Alice Springs, Bangladesh /
I understand complex emotional systems /
My mother was my childhood dog, run over before she was
born, so don't tell me about sorrow /

I grew up on a hay bale propped atop the Himalayas in the
Mexican state of Kaikohe, Kazakhstan /
The stories are true I've nothing to hide /
My mother was my childhood dog, run over before she was
born /
Lenny Kravitz, Prince, Jimi Hendrix, all fabulous lovers /

The stories are true   I've nothing to hide /
See how I relate /
Prince, Jimi Hendrix, Barack Obama, Scarlet & Frank O'Hara /
Poetry & politics are in the blood /

See how I relate /

Max, my great great great uncle, shtetl heartthrob & political activist, was arrested in 1895, thrown into a Russian jail & Rose, the aunt on the outside, sang in Yiddish through the bars /

Poetry & politics my darlings, some things are in the blood /
Rebellion is in the blood /

I may have mentioned Max, arrested in 1895 & thrown into a Russian jail & Rose who sang in Yiddish through the bars & the guards thought: harmless lullaby but it was actually an escape plan /

Folks, I care, oh my god I care /
Rebellion is in my blood /
Send me to jail if you wish, for I believe in many things /

I care, oh my god I care /
I nurture my mythologies as robustly as you shelter to yours /
Send me to jail if you wish, for I'll believe in anything /
But come election day do consider my singular story /

Embrace my mythologies & I shall acknowledge yours /
Vote for me, blood of Max, jailed for his politics & of Rose who broke him out with a lullaby /
Come election day do consider my inspiring story /
My mother's mother's mother left Russia for America & became the first female pharmacist in New York City /

Imagine: Max, jailed for his political beliefs & Rose who broke him out with a lullaby /
Then this pharmacy, which before long becomes a front for

dealing heroin to the mob /
My mother's mother's mother was the first female pharmacist in NYC /
These are facts   We have the news clippings /

& yes her pharmacy was a front for dealing heroin to the mob /
See this photo of her in a frilly white dress, wide-brimmed hat & enormous gun strapped to her side /
These are facts   We have the news clippings /
What is my point   Dear audience /

There is the photo of my great-grandmother with an enormous machine gun strapped to her side /
But my point is not about organised crime /
What is my point /
My point is that I come from well connected & fearless & entrepreneurial stock /

My point is not of homogenised time /
I have no ghosts /
I come from well connected & fearless & entrepreneurial stock /
Justin Trudeau still sends chocolates   See how I shake out the sheets /

I have no ghosts /
My opponents will argue that the timeline meanders but I shall fire back /
Dorothy Gale has the other half of this locket   See how I shake out the sheets /
History is a game of Broken Telephone /

I shall fire back /
Plotlines curl & twist, are dropped, picked up later,
repurposed or rewritten /
Mystery is a game of Token Xylophone /
Edges fray & are mended with new perspective /

Plotlines twist & curl, are dropped, picked up later,
repurposed or rebitten /
What does it matter if there are embellishments /
Pledges stray & are blended with blue perspex lids /
Who doesn't relish some abstraction now & then /

What does it matter if there are embellishments /
Homer, the Bible, *Lord of the Rings* /
Who doesn't relish a metaphor now & then /
If it's good it might as well count /

Homer, the Bible, Harry Potter /
I ask you   define reality to your neighbour & you will each
come up with different answers /
If it's good it might as well count /
A show of hands, please, how many of you chose the vial of
blood over the Stradivarius /

Define reality to your neighbour & you will each come up
with different answers /
Did I mention I am   so well connected /
A show of hands   how many of you chose the Stradivarius
over the message in a bottle /
It's true   my great great uncle Joachim was violinist to the
Tsar /

Vote for me, I am   so well connected /

A position I would indeed consider reinstating should I be elected in September /

Is that of my great great uncle Joachim   violinist to the Tsar /

Ah but Sam, I hear you say, everyone's Russian great-grandmother was potentially Anastasia /

Look, there are positions I would indeed consider reinstating should I be elected /

I have the receipts   I didn't want to have to show them but ok, if you insist, I will bring the receipts /

Ah but Sam, you say, every Hamilton kōtiro is secretly a Tainui princess, & yes, ok, I hear you /

& positively argue that a vote for me is a vote for dreaming & old photographs /

Friends, I have the receipts   I guarantee 100% you will not want to miss when I unveil the receipts /

Ok   fireside time   Colleagues, countryfolk /

Regarding dreaming & these old photographs /

Remember in the war when I saved your sorry arse /

Friends, colleagues, countryfolk /

I'm no hero /

But remember in the war when I taught that yoga class /

I've had my struggles   You know, with self-esteem /

Some call me a hero /

Of humble beginnings, yes /

I've had my struggles /

My grandfather was found with his infant siblings beside their
dead mother /

Humble beginnings /
My grandmother was held by the ankle out the window by a
wicked woman /
My grandfather & his infant siblings gurgling on the kitchen
floor beside their dead blind mother /
My uncle saved his ice creams so his mother could have a lick
Now he's a real-estate tycoon /

My grandmother was dangled by the ankle out of a window
by Philip Pullman /
But look at us now /
My uncle is a real hate typhoon /
My father was nominated for the Best Dream Prize & my
mother is a shaman /

Look at us now /
My brother really did find treasure on an island & my sister
has the president's number /
My father was dominated by surprise & my mother is a
ploughman /
Vote for me /

My brother really did find pleasure of a kind & my sister is
the resident plumber /
When I was a child, I drew rainbow-coloured orchestras /
Vote for me /
& the gorgeous lies that we wrap around ourselves in order to
have one step follow the next /

When I was a child, I had a rainbow-coloured orchestra /
Friends, hands up if you remember your dreams /
Art, poetry   such gorgeous elegant lies that we wrap around
ourselves /
Vote for me & I'll insist they count   & recount   Till we
win /

Friends, sing out if you remember your dreams /
Oh, sweet constituents   I love you like you were one of my
own numerous & successful daughters /
Vote for me & I'll insist you count & recount   Till we win
/
Congratulations /

Sweet constituents I love you like you were one of my own
very numerous & successful racehorses /
We are winners, we have won, we are fabulous winners who
have already won /
Congratulations /
Yes, I am still so very velveteen /

We are winners, we have won, we are fabulous winners who
have already won /
& soon, perhaps I shall return to the ocean /
Tell me, am I not still very velveteen /
My advice   go to bed   upon waking, write it down /

Soon, perhaps I shall return to the ocean /
That mighty ballot box /
Till then, go to bed   upon waking, write it down   repeat /
I am incredibly wealthy & devastatingly handsome & really
good at sports /

See you at the ballot box /
Remember my everyman's story /
I am incredibly healthy & devastatingly handy & really good
at thoughts   but you know this /
I am relatable   I am a very distinguished shame   Vote for
me /

(We hear, misinterpret, then depart.) —Manhire

—Ken Bolton

Dedications

To Anita: complete with scissors and buttons
For Donovan: a lesson
To Christopher: humming a little tune
For Neil: we tried
To Jack: a pasture of hens
For Ngaire: her cloudy head
For my grandfather: the standard question
For Amy: empty nutshells
To Janet: harder than quartz

Follow Up

I have some questions, Sam

Go on

My question is how did it go with the guy
　　　did you learn all the names of the trees?

My question is regarding these artificial crowds
　　　did you kiss critical mass?

My question is are you still subtly whoring
　　　is that song finally out of your head?

My question is do you still laugh at your neighbour
　　　have you learned to love?

Question: is everything funny
　　　or are we better for sadder reasons?

My question is more birds? as is the tired national custom?
　　　any thoughts on sports?

My question is once again twofold
　　　before you skipped town did you mow the lawn
　　　& do you think anybody cared?

Boy Oh Boy Oh Boy Oh Boy

as a last-ditch campaign in the countryside
one might rise from the kitchen table to
make a whole lot of lions
/
for kindness   protection   devilry
one can always make lions!
as they did in the Dark Ages
/
& today
                bewildering noon
there is a sort of lightness
/
despite
you know
all the reasons
/
Sometimes
everything is miraculous   miraculous
alive as black mould
/
Sometimes
everything is very still
you make a lion
/
you say
   that's good

Memory!

The dicks are out
Out on the tables
Enormous dicks

Everyone leaning across each other stroking all the dicks
Calling out to me, c'mon have a stroke of these dicks!
It's nice!

&

I have learned
to not listen
to hum a little tune

I have learned
to hum
to pop a log on the fire even now with spring on the way

I have learned
to be happy
& warm

I have learned
to break a window
neatly with no blood

I have learned
to say 'you have a terrible anger problem!'
then to chuckle

at my heroism
It's funny
I'm being funny

I have learned
to be funny
to delight in all of our

separate
various
unravellings

I have learned
to sing when the dicks are out: show tunes
They do recoil at show tunes!

. . . when confronted with a daddish waif
who doesn't mind waggling a finger
& who laughs at his own unspoken jokes

& who might turn suddenly on his heel
& sing
Ooooooooooooooklahoma!

some dicks do recoil . . .
at Oklahoma . . .
& you know   I find myself feeling 'lighter in the loafers'

Am I using this phrase correctly?
I find I do/don't care
if I am using things correctly

I have learned
that when cornered there is often little time
to consider whether this or that is correct so you just belt out

Tomorrow
Tomorrow
I'll love ya, tomorrow

& they leave
usually
the dicks . . .

. . . tho sometimes
& I am still learning . . .
they bite my face

. . . sight of a peacock makes me sick

—Charlie Darwin

The Embryo Repeats

1

Ah yes, Monday / & here is God now / in God's slippers / in God's kitchen / looking in God's pantry / slits chords tails / good / great / God mixes up a base for a few of the usual tchotchkes / Fishes Ants / God really has a / really superb collection / Really so many fishes & ants & lots of other fishy anty things / Beetles Clouds / Ferns Squids / God always says *know your bases* / & God's bases are wide & complex / God's bases are fair & dispersed / God's bases poke the atmosphere / God's bases knead the core / Today God mixes up a slitty chordy taily base / simmers till clear & then / cos God's still in 7th day mode / God hoicks up a lurgy stirs it in cos fuck it, right? & God / pops the base into a segmented tray & leaves it to set at optimal temp / & God is one of these creatives who gets bored quickly / Show God a quetzal & God will be like ugh my quetzal phase / God is always looking for the new movie of God's life / hence God's CV rainforests / oceans / stars / & cos of this God can sometimes be a little bit of a shit / hence the morning's hoick / Well by noon God's sabotage has metastasized & God's kitchen is a mess / quetzal feathers are everywhere / & God's base is a magnificent crumbling palace fabulous unfiltered sun purple triple shadow / & God's bases are *always* gaudy open systems ripe & pumping giddily towards entropy with lush interpretive margins / in which / A resides / & this time A has clocked a cracking / A picks up a long green feather chews the fleshy tip / A might embrace a glacier yeah / A might leave a charcoal wake / & God shall fall back into God's chair & watch everything come tumbling down / down down down

2

Who is that speaking / Who is that, down the hall, singing in the shower / Who is that speaking / Who is that, on a train, pressing a thumb into a thigh / Who is that speaking / Who is that, turning in the street, at night, in a soft rain / Who is that speaking / Who is that, at the blackboard, present & unasked & ready

3

C shimmers from banners, trickles thru anecdote, pumps in dreams / amen / *God's star-shaped heart, God's confetti-stuffed mouth / amen* / C under lights, steps like this   like this   &   like   this / amen / *God's glossy lip, God's tender flank / amen* / C comes at God with scissors, snips fast till God's closely shorn / amen / *God's flooded breast, God's breathless cheer / amen* / C sparkles, precise as mathematics / amen / *God's love, God's terror / amen* / C smoulders, retreats, but it's art when C does / amen / *God's terror, God's trust / amen* / C takes the scissors to God, lops God's head right off, fixes it to a new thing / amen / *God's blessed turn / amen* / headless God sags & grows pale / amen / *lemmings, wildebeests, rats, bees, starlings in a sack / amen* / the new headed thing cries for attention & to be loved, flushes pastel, ripples like a cuttlefish / amen / *wisps of smoke / amen* / C breathes God in & exhales horses cities planets mythology lust / amen / *God's informed position / amen* / C eyeballs God, smooth & tidy as a nut / amen / *God's jagged eye, electric neck, throbbing for the pop / amen* / C takes a balletic leap / *God's relief   God's blood-spattered exhaustion   hallelujah hallelujah   amen*

4

an ancient knotty trunk / curled around boulders / bent by the wind / squinting in the wind / shoulders up against the wind / the wind passes over like a firm hand on a cat / D tingles smooth as fur

Old clothes made the mouse / (pbu old clothes) / Mud made the crocodile / (pbu mud) / Meat made the fly / (pbu meat) / & so / when medieval sailors / after puzzling over the disappearance each September of all the little birds / brought up nets of empty oyster shells / it followed / swallows were amphibious / & hatched on the ocean floor / pearlescent husks / left for netting / & fledglings / bursting like tiny marlins / across probing bows / Proof / E is charming & creative / E is a thinker & / good at building things / E likes to renovate & elucidate as E hammers / Slave ships in the seventeenth & eighteenth centuries crossing the Atlantic tossed pregnant women overboard / E has many choice factoids on phenomena difficult to understand / Eels are born from dewdrops / (pbu dewdrops) / E suggests it's obvious once you know / In the meantime someone's gotta clean up God's great mess! / & E is the F for the job / F should throw all F's empty tins & other trash into the infinite yard / F is useful / You should thank F / pbu F

6

It's a performance / this whole living gag / & G does have a face for it!   /   a nice face   /   God reflects   /   a nice recognisable face / & God thinks how G's smile really 'lights up a room' / God admires how G will sit on the edge of G's bed driving nails through G's toes / really bashing like at a jammed door & yet / still going on to step out of an evening / & everyone always saying   how glamorous

7

they love me / they love me / they cut a pomegranate / they cry but it's a kind of living when they do / & when they come they'll have a big tree to cry under & tall grass to cry in & a soft hammock to cry from & a high high high bird to cry at & a sturdy lap to cry into & a cool hall to recover in & a little pomegranate jube to suck   as a prize / they love me / they love me / & after the baby's been put to bed   everybody will dance in the kitchen

8

How is I distinguished from the other animals? / I wishes to drive a small car fast / *Imagination distinguishes I from the other animals* / I has found a spider's web & doesn't know which way to love it / *Meanwhile the deserts* / I suggests God recovers God's head from the Mariana Trench / *Ah but language, famously, distinguishes I from the other animals!* / I turns towards I's neighbour, beams, touches hands, feels familial, linked! / *discounting the bird songs we love & the whale songs we love & the bee dances we admire & the ape laughs we recognise* / I scrawls I's stories on bathroom stalls & believes they are I's own / I breeds out the wolf by selecting for cute & believes it is I's own / Everywhere is comic books & babies

9

Zebras murder their stepchildren so tell me   how is J distinguished from the other animals?   /   God needs to back the fuck off cos J is trying real real hard not to grow into a particular thing tho that bloody path is so lush

10

K wakes behind a Vaseline gel & begins calling everything
Honey   /   Pets & trees & blocks of cheese   /   the laundry
casserole   parcel / Speak to me / Honey   Honey? / Tell
me what you want / K is a deep & calloused toll / K is a
shimmer / a serious cloud / valuable / brief / K is God
brand honey leaking from God's saved paper bag   /   a
satisfactory redolence left over so many proto nouns
/ K shall manifest a good fleshy noun / K shall manifest an
original good fleshy noun with many syllables

11

& behold L the baby / M the mother / N the photo passed
around / O our interrogation

12

God was thinking   I'll destroy them all / But before God
could get to killing   P saw a couple fucking / very close to
hallowed ground / So P   a Zealot   killed the couple / &
God thought ah well cancel that   /   & God said l'chayim P
for taking one for the team / & since P was so Zealous & had
scratched God's bloody itch   God thought a small blessing
in order   /   So God said P most loyal servant   you are so
Zealous etcetera   & I really   respect your Zeal / &
God began to grant the blessing   /   But here God became
frustrated / Cos God was supposed to do the killing! / Plus P
had killed this couple for engaging in arguably the holiest of
acts / Tho remember / P was a Zealot / & God appreciated
Zealousy / So whatever / God gave P the blessing / But a
sideways blessing / With an important bit in miniature / &
the miniature bit   is God mumbling / is God clearing God's
throat   /   is God acknowledging that God & some of God's
creations   are a little   hmm   cray cray / & then with a
broken vav for shalom   P is left with an imperfect brucha /
Kicked across the way / Sorry not sorry / Sly compromise /
War / Shrug / Peace / Yeah / Everything is fine

13

God is the word for a funeral / God is the same word for a
wedding / God is this word for a dying bird who gets married
& then dies / God is the word for a strong broad wing
feather / God is the word for a small soft chest feather / &
Q *loves* God / & Q wants to be so very close to God / & Q
says the word many times in order to bring God close / &
God lets Q pluck one feather for every utterance / & God is
glad to gift Q so many soft broad feathers / & God thinks
I am beloved / & God thinks   Q is happy / but I have so
few feathers left   God thinks   I have so few feathers left /
I have so few feathers left / Friends   my skin is showing

14

God hugs R for 5 minutes in a dream / God hugs R so tight
/ God loves R   in a dream   & they hug / God hugs this
thing with the juddery eye / once on a peninsula / & later
in the kitchen / they are generous with their hugging / they
recognise it is a dream   God thinks / & are generous

15

Every stone leaf petal twig & breeze claw wave mote
thunderclap   makes up the great black box of God & S can't
piss in public /

T escapes / T slips quietly out the back / T slips out the back of God &   into the shiny night / T slips out & under & holds T's breath so God can't see / when God shines a torch over God's still black surface   God can't see / T holds T's breath T holds it & holds it / T tumbles along gently like a careful log / & the night pays T no heed / so T hangs out there for a couple of years / moving slowly / resting in the mud or on a rock / baby nights gathering to watch T   wide eyed as handfuls of loosely drawn tarsiers / till one day T gets nipped on the leg & the   urge for daylight becomes so real T decides to make a run for it / smashes a downstairs window & all the mud the rocks the logs the night come spilling out in a torrent   leaving behind a crumpled red corrugated iron pile   damp   & stinking &   empty / kids hang out in those rusted ruins now / getting high & recollecting

17

U came upon a field & saw it was a field / U came upon a
valley & saw it was a valley / U came upon a mountain & saw
it was   so mountainous / U felt a hot wind blow & knew
U was up to a   bad circling / U grew sticky & began to
unwrap Uself like a frustrated baby / U cast off U's casings &
strode   towards the gorgeous void / & U   & the void
locked eyes / U saw Boy & Whale flirting in a shallow / U
saw Lion & Stag   rutting in a meadow / U saw the easy
corralling of magnificent ease / U came upon a number of
ghosts   emerging from sawdust / U came upon
congregations   swollen & rosy with denial / U came upon
Dancing & saw that it was Praying / U came upon Crying &
saw that it was Living / U came upon Living & saw that it
was Lying / U leapt at the sound of gunfire   but it was only
a thousand starlings / U felt U's mouth   move in U's hands
like that of a   large fish / U   came upon a door

What is this what is this   V is radiant with curiosity / &
God's silence   is so   competitive / but what is it what is it
/ God pats God's pockets   God seems to have lost God's
scorecard / C'mon God srsly   V is bulging V is luminous
with discovery / So God cans the charade & catches V
one-handed & flicks V up   into an unadorned night sky &
rare nocturnal W's mark it in their diaries /

new moon

19

How is X distinguished from the other animals? / X keeps a particular prayer tucked in X's bumbag / *How is X distinguished from the other animals?* / X drunk-texts God said prayer once or twice a week / *How is X distinguished from the other animals?* / In the 90s the town of Houtouwan was abandoned by its citizens & promptly forgotten   In less than 20 years the village was reclaimed entirely by nature   The buildings & streets are now cloaked in greenery & tourists pay $3 each to stand on a platform & take photos / *How is X distinguished from the other animals?* / God chuckles   God sighs & shakes God's head   God wipes away God's tear

Time / Y is calling time / Y has made many renovations /
& God says ok then / God will remove Y from the schedule
/ & God leads Y through theatres cloakrooms landings / &
God folds Y up under a stairwell & instructs Y to wait there to
be remembered / & Y is found by a boy with slender brown
feet & eyes that look like he just woke up but will one day
look like laughing / & Y bursts gently from stairwells
landings theatres cloakrooms foyers carparks & out to a coast
& hundreds of penguins / Gentoos & Adélies holding hands
/ Emperors & rockhoppers sharing secrets / Chinstraps &
little blues unwrapping lunch / Y sinks back into hot grey
sand & considers Paradise / Then a slender brown foot taps
Y on the ankle & the sleepy boy says   hello Old Chip / & Y
curls like burning paper / & Y's ashes cling to the dewy sex
of stunted karamu & the boy thinks   ha   déjà vu / &
catches up with his friends   laughing /

Allemande in G by J.S. Bach

Bars 1–17 transposed & arranged by S.L. Duckor-Jones

Allegro moderato

Bars 1–3

Bring!   giantdoggybags . . . ! Advance gammy franknesses
Gloom desists eternally for   geodes and borrowed charms /
Demonstrative bicycles go flop   Get edgy   Do chummy
bourgeois caricatures   Dote earnestly   Forgive gavotting
alumni boastings /

Bars 4–6

Coughing at glamorous fêtes   gags even frumpy gentlemen
and decadent freebasing gags   aloof bipartisan crowds and /
believability gags gently defensive   dolts Be beatific Gag
generously . . . Buy!   ablenderCream! babes and ghouls / at
bachelor cribs and   gloat freshly Get a   dealer . . . car
Bang angels Get festooned /

Bars 7–9

Gain eternal elevation Bounce   back Gain grace Examine
elevation . . . Boys   elevate gains from america / Gain
friction Elevate friction   Gain choices Gather forecasted
general choices earmarked for   gains Expenditure and gross
/ Forecasts . . . damned eternal   forecasts dredging gleeful
elevations   Flub direction Forecast glowing   aunties
baking cakes awhile /

Bars 10–12

Bread Doughy grainy decadent   bread Good and fresh
Got eggs Got avocado   Bread could define breakfast /
Can't eat avocados excluding   carbs and bread does
count as do buns   Can anyone enjoy gluten / free . . . egg
free dough   Aging gentry fancy eating   dolloped alligator
gelatin Even   for dinner Antiquated cunts /

Bars 13–15

Blind . . . accounts can go   deep Can bring about   genuine
demonic change and   boost good demons for / country
god and bone   Chattier demons eventually fade   Guys act
cool Don't   eviscerate a good . . . / demon Golf for
everyone   For dads aunts daughters   Don't fret A chill
bitch . . . awaits /

Bars 16–17

Glancedismissivelybackwards . . . at   golden fools earning
dollars   cents Earning actual gold   Fussing daily Assessing
credit / daily . . . Absconding   daily Fingering alien
commodities   daily Asking for dick   daily /
repeat

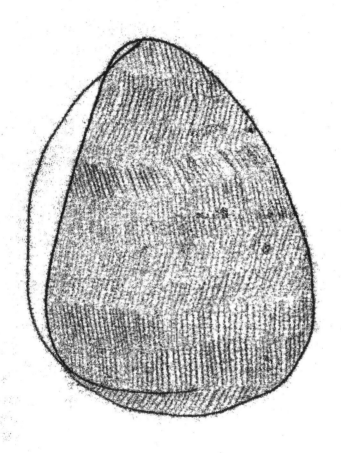

Oh Felicia,
where the fuck are we?

—Bernadette Bassenger

Dear Citizen

do you intend to read the news . do you intend to visit your
father . how much bubble wrap is required? . do you intend to
prepare a soufflé . do you intend to hand over your heart .
how much bubble wrap is required? . we're running low . we
need to know . how much bubble wrap is required?

Dear Resident

there will be a 15-minute public fireworks display at 9pm on May 14 to mark Yom Ha'atzmaut . the Jerusalem City Council advises that any popping banging and/or whizzing between 9 and 9:15 on the evening of May 14 is most likely to be fireworks . the Jerusalem City Council acknowledges that such exuberances may paint an anxious aural picture for many re current events . the Jerusalem City Council suggests residents cast their minds back to basic training to distinguish the sounds of Yom Ha'atzmaut from that of war . the Jerusalem City Council has already engaged in such self reflection and supposes that fireworks make a rather deep 'hobgoblin' while gunfire sounds like 'I-did-it I-did-it' and bombs give a sort of short shallow 'DAMN' . residents might like to jot these descriptions down onto a post-it and pop the post-it on the fridge . the JCC gives a shout-out to those living near to but outside of town and expects they may see on the night of May 14 an ominous glow on the horizon . the Jerusalem City Council advises that this will merely be from the Yom Ha'atzmaut festivities and that the Holy City is probably* not under attack . in addition the Jerusalem City Council suggests all citizens pick up any loose pieces of bubble wrap that may have fallen to the floor before carrying fragile bodies and/or minds across the room, until further notice

Dear Izzy

you were supposed to be a great global light . even as a kid so famous already . so smart so good-looking . all that attention did it go to your head . oh Izzy a plucky charm has metastasized & I can't be your friend anymore . we believed in you Izzy . when under your sun we took off our clothes ate your oranges in your oases . wriggled through your tunnels with candles in our teeth . danced in your deserts with your sandy-eyed children & next morning high on holiness poked our prayers between your stones . we were like *Izzy! oh my god* . but these days Izzy honey . there is nothing courageous about threatening the weak & I can't be your friend anymore . I know you're hurting & frightened but lashing out isn't the answer . all it does is sting the rest of us . turns us into strangers you know? . maybe this is your rock-bottom Izzy . if you want to get better we will help you get better but first you need to acknowledge you have a problem ok? till then I am throwing up my hands enough . enough enough enough . & enough with these new friends . hateful Utah loons . why do you associate with such thugs? it's embarrassing . it's destructive . people ask me what's up with Izzy & I say I just don't know . I have no answers . I sigh I shrug . I say we used to be friends . Izzy today you are nobody's light & that is such a shame . *I know* there are laughing free gays in Magen David's playing volleyball on your beaches & I'd love for that to define you . but it's difficult to make out those sweet boys through all your door-slamming name-calling self-harm & bulldozing . how disappointing to be defined by ugliness . get it together Izzy . we miss our friend, sincerely.

Bumper Holiday Mega Quiz

1. How is this man a light unto all the other nations?
2. How is this night distinguished from all other animals?
3. How is this nation different from all the other nights?
4. Are you my mother?

One point if you answered
my friends make a lot of money working in shiny buildings

Two points if you answered
my friends are poor but they are shiny mansions unto themselves

Five points if you answered
I love all of my friends equally, at times

Ten points if you answered
it's ok to be merely sateen at home watching others shine on TV

A hundred points if you answered
the saddest thing about vacuuming is damning all the little bits of shine
to an eternity amongst dust

A thousand points if you answered
here have this piece of tinfoil I found in the grass

A million points if you answered
I'm thinking of getting my ears pierced, I walk down the street, thinking
& thinking

Five-Thousand-Year Quiz

Q: *Josh is idealistically broke on a beach with a dozen free rabbis who have no qualms about uplifting watermelons: where did they come from? these watermelons? these watermelons these rabbis these pigeons?*

A: we all want to live here! but not as it is! BLOOM we chant! plant oaks! put some chicks in! make it look like Babu's back yard! fill the yellow dunes with oranges –

Q: *no water, no water!?*

A: – but we'll weep so abundantly upon touchdown the stricken sea will be resurrected & we'll pump her again as prophesised! make those grapefruits shudder so dewily you'd think we were in a Ugandan valley after all!

Q: *& these pigeons – where did they come from & what do they want & can we send them back?*

A: we wrap ourselves in keffiyehs *NO!* & vomit in the shallows keep on coming lads keep on coming all over these stones they want it I swear you just can't hear cos the manna from heaven is in your ears . . .

Top rate
100%

*a kilometre away was the Clarence River and above that
mountains of two thousand feet . . .
and the noise of the boulders splashing into the river
and the dust
the dust was something you'd never
you'd never imagine to see
and the willow trees and the poplar trees that surrounded the old hut . . .
eighty feet high and
cracking like stock whips
It was a noise I'd never heard before . . .
and I've heard a lot of noises . . .
and seen chimneys come down but this was exceptional, so
you can imagine . . .

When there's nothing to do,
do nothing

—Karen Kamensek

Plan A

shave beard
reveal self to be
broad, like a swimmer
stand on stage
say nothing
be beloved

19/9

Not FINANCE,
FINE ARTS

said the check-out girl to
the chatty man &

she handed him his
pumpkin

Postcards

Dear _____ we waited forty-five
minutes for the best
cream puffs in
Sydney

Dear ____ you are & have
always been the best
cream puff in
Sydney

11/8

Peter
looking beautiful in a scarf
walking home around the bays

Plan B

the Waimarie has gone
it's ok

I never expected
to find

my true love in
Whanganui

(end)

Truth, I don't even know what is the truth
after all these lies I have told

—Sophie Zawistowski

True Stories

██████ & hair the dark of brown that's cousin to magenta
After he left I googled hot Indians & went to bed for a while
Fellahs   it's a lonely pill but   it's constant as hell & that's
██████████   When a dog tore the back off of one of his chooks
T took that chook & plopped it down & backed his car right
over it   Beethoven in the tapedeck   this retelling   may
have ████████████ Truth   a kererū flew through the
doorway   I looked square into that little red eye before she
spun around   that pigeon flew straight through my door
broke a cup frightened the dog   so what   so what if I
don't have a ████ I'm my own wishy-washy media machine
a falsehood of R-rated whimsy & carefully selected naturalist
beats   I tell my overseas relatives that artists live in this
town   & ██████████ The first time K climbed into my
bed I said dude we've been here before   I've lain with you a
hundred times   I've been to the opera in Sydney with H
I've wrestled a whale on Eastbourne Beach   I remember
████████████ Holocaust memorial service   We listen to a
man recall dinner in the ghetto   Potato peelings from the
gutter   The man cries & we all stand up   Proclaim that
we'll Never Forget   & D leans over whispers to me   *but*
memory's a ████████████████████████████████████
██████████ Great flocks of kererū block out the midday sun

12:55 to Masterton

. . . but he always was a smart arse //

                The way he'd treat me in the shop

. . . smart arse // //

                      Big dope smoker //   // I saw him
                      drunk once   round Shelly Bay
                  I thought you judge us //
                  Like all pot smokers //   //
                  he thought he was superior //
             He said   we're totally mortgage-free
                      I said   good on ya //
                  He said   we travel every year
                      I said   good on ya //

. . . but are they classy // //
. . . she was classy //

                She brought nice bags back from Vegas //
                              Look //
                          Fashion Week
                    We should go // // //
                      // and to Italy
. . . Italy // Classy // the Italians // //
. . . or France // // // // // //

              No   France is dangerous now
. . . and not at our age //

But we'll go somewhere   //   //
We'll save some money   //
Christchurch   //   or something

. . . I was thinking Sydney   but then I thought
. . . never   //   //   //
. . . never never never

It's alright to   cry at a funeral   //
. . . you enjoy it   //   //

You enjoy it //

//   //
The day David died
my life became a struggle
//   //   //   //   //   //   //

Sage Advice

these are not my own words
Jacob became exceedingly afraid & was distressed
He was anxious & worried regarding himself
& Fear demonstrates lack of trust

Jacob became exceedingly afraid & was distressed
Once Jacob realised that he feared Esau, he became anxious
His Fear demonstrating a lack of trust
The limit of his trust caused him anxiety, for he reasoned that
    he was not worthy

Once Jacob realised that he feared Esau, he became anxious
He confused what is true: "I am afraid", with a story about an
    imagined outcome
The limit of his trust caused him anxiety, for he reasoned that
    he was not worthy
What if Jacob could have: named what was arising

Jacob confused what is true: "I am afraid" with a story about
    an imagined outcome
What if Jacob had simply noted: "this is what fear feels like"
    & allowed it to exist
What if Jacob could have: named what was arising
These are not my own words

Word

I was a chief in Ethiopia   What do you think about that?
Learning in school about Lenin & Marx   In English
In Ethiopia   When the Soviets fell we laughed   We laughed
at all the marble statues of Lenin in Ethiopia   I'm of
semitic heritage   So I know   Courteney Cox Shakira
Michelle Obama   I know   Trump Apollo   I know
I was a chief in Ethiopia & now   I'm a born again
New Zealander   Māori stories!   Knowledge!   I want it!
I want to know!   Reading is leading   But equality
Gaddafi   had a green book just like   Chairman Mao
had a red one   Equality   Listen

We are equal like the teeth of a jackass

Different Sides of the Man

This is the Jew symbolically
>>> somewhere in the night
>>> handcuffs, balcony, blouse, brocade . . .
>>> his name in misty light

This is the Jew metaphorically
>>> somewhere in the night
>>> a collection of imagined things . . .
>>> his name in southern light

This is the Jew obliquely
>>> somewhere in the night
>>> estranged, showing the back style . . .
>>> his name in folding light

This is the Jew physically
>>> somewhere in the night
>>> no time for love, but everyone loves . . .
>>> his name in wounded light

This is the Jew practically
>>> somewhere in the night
>>> sliding into a deep purple jacket . . .
>>> his name in homemade light

This is the Jew instrumentally
>>> somewhere in the night
>>> he appears, he gives the right answers . . .
>>> his name in serious light

This is the Jew primarily
                    somewhere in the night
                 . sitting alone in his car &
                              this large balloon was launched &
                              the the wind was really howling &
                              the phone booth in the rain
                              The storm . . .

This is the Jew simply
                    somewhere in the night   best
                    getaway
                    driver in the
                    business . . .

Wage Advice

David is just living her life

Moshe says: an abundance

*

David: maybe tonight skip the TV show and sit down to talk about money

Levi: you do get men who must have a new car very often

Yigal: or whatever

Golda: a little trip down to Whakatāne's fine for me

Yitzhak R: fish 'n' chips & supermarket plonk

Menachem: it's not stupid to get a little counselling

Yitzhak S: I wish people would try a little bit more with numbers

Shimon: when you say that you sound like a bit of a worry but anyway, moving on

Yitzhak S: I was out walking the other day & I thought how can I explain this & I thought about asparagus

Yitzhak R: bunches of asparagus

Shimon: in the depths of winter when there's no asparagus around it might cost ten dollars for a bunch

Benjamin: the asparagus analogy works to some extent, but with asparagus you're eating it right away, you're not worried about the future of asparagus, you're just thinking today this is what it costs and I'm going to have it for dinner

Ehud B: it's an approximation but it's pretty close to correct

Ariel: for listeners listening to this and saying what the hell is she going on about, it's not something that you need to know, just an interesting thing

*

Ehud O is just living her life

Benjamin says: I recommend you don't take much notice

No.1 to Island Bay

you're a god   you're a god

says our rush-hour prophet   swaying yeastily from the
handrail   sinking softly into his hi-vis   recollecting
anointments   while we his stony-faced flock   finger our
receipts   flowers, bread

you're a god   you're a god

he whispers   *. . . you're a god*

& his sister   she's a god too   & he casts a spell on the
traffic   & a German girl talks about school with a Japanese
girl across the aisle   & a woman says   *around six thirty* &
a man says   *great great*   &

ooooo weee!

our visionary flops down sweetly   into a free seat   shaking
his head   closing his eyes   & insisting quietly till the end of
the line

you're gods   you're all gods

O Man

All of it, far gone. Hello?
This is your mother. Are you
Coming home?

All of us, far gone.
Mister? . . .
. . . Mother?

All of us by violence.
Hello? Is anybody there? To her friends:
These kids with their activities, and she wept then, too.

For all of us by violence died.
Mister, our mothers used to say, I beg of you
Please choose something.

But for all – I said Mister, said our mothers, I took
My baby by the shoulders, I tried
To find their eyes with my eyes, but far gone were they.

For all of us by violence died, far gone
In sin until the last hour, when the blaze
Of Heaven's light brought understanding.

Our mothers now, at reddy pools, in the quiet part,
And the blaze of Heaven's light bringing only
Howling and silhouettes and silhouettes that howl hello.

Hello? Our mothers fall against each other,
They slump before our bits that still glisten in the blaze
With necessary deceit . . . we just lay down. Mother?

Mister, this is your mother, have you met a nice one?
Are you coming home?
I understand. I don't understand.

Hello? I left a message. I left it under the
Blaze of Heaven's light, in the last hour of my walk.
It may bring understanding.

Sin, son,
But then please phone, tell me all about it.
This is your mother.

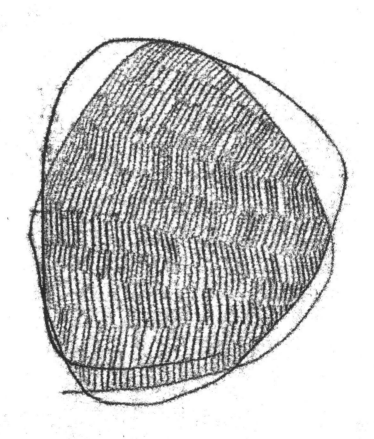

Allemande in G by J.S. Bach

Bars 18–34 transposed & arranged by S.L. Duckor-Jones

Bars 18–19
Actually / David avenged ... Frida Greta avenged David
Erin fought Glen   avenged Fiona divorced Callum /

Bars 20–22
Basketball does good for   Glen and basketball challenges
David Basketball and Greta   fit easily Fiona dribbles /
Erin ... dives Can   Callum catch David Erin debates club
basketball Callum   debates basketball casually and /
David ... fetches Erins   basketball deftly calls bullshit
clears Erin fistbumps Greta   and Callum backs away /

Bars 23–25
David ... brings Callum   devilled eggs Frida brings
Greta ... eggs   Benedict David comes back / Asks Erin
carefully ... bring   a guy five eggs   folded dipped baked
and   bound Callum doesn't agree / Greta agrees barely Erin
feigns disgust Callum bawls   ceaselessly Eggs are broken
Erin begins ... anew /

Bars 26–28
About eleven am ... bells   chime bringing Callum galloping
for Glen and Erin   David coos bobbing awkwardly / Glen
decides Fiona could   be a genius and   beckons Callum
dockside Erin   documents everything Fiona eats /
Eventually ... Greta ...   comes clean bearing apples
Apples burnished calm effective   Don't ... cry /

Bars 29–31

David's . . . anecdote . . .   belies Callum's bloody account
Glen forgets Erin's gift   Birthdays don't count Birthdays /
come . . . gradually . . .   Birthdaygirl Erin fakes gratitude
Fiona argues birthday code   David condones birthdays and
/ Greta defends Fiona and   Callum assesses Fiona's defence
Greta demurs blushingly . . . David   eventually gags and
collapses /

Bars 32–34

David and Fiona elongate   Dammit Fiona Greta barks
can't Greta ever dominate   Coolly Erin assesses chaos /
Frida accentuates chaos Erin   deserts . . . chaos   Because
Glen aggravates Greta   David assumes Glen fucked / Greta
Greta berates David   Glen berates David Frida   glows
Deserves better Gets   Glen
repeat

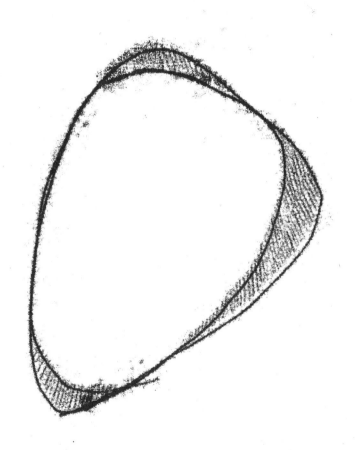

Real comes and goes and isn't very interesting

—Dr Ruth-Anne Tibbets

HI!

Pay no attention to the man behind the curtain . . .
Just kidding! please pay me lots of attention!
What's that? oh you know
I've just been doodling
here in my loft:

Plans for roller coasters
Plans for absconding
Plans for an online jewellery campaign
Plans for death and marriage
Plans for the Paris Opera Ballet, note to self, check messages

Excuse the mess
I wasn't expecting guests
But that's another joke
I expect you
always

Deep Time

After   the vacuum cleaner broke
down he   decided to stop all
cleaning so   the wooden floors now
ripple with   the marks of toes &
heels like   a ski field from the ski
lift or   paper dance instructions
Pausing   naked in the living room
he needn't   close the curtains
The dusty panes   are quite opaque
All a passerby   might see is the
glow of his red lamp   shade Layer
of dust upon layer of dust   rooms
swell & shift like sand dunes till his
dwelling space becomes   so small
he has to go outside   to stretch his
arms   see   the   sky

Scientists a thousand years from now,
drilling for core samples, will
pinpoint the time when his vacuum
broke down & he stopped cleaning
altogether.   How it affected the
environment, adjacent life forms, etc,
etc.   Such data is so valuable for
forecasting future slumps.

Night

boy peels back blue wallpaper
comfy navy scab   picked as he falls asleep
this blister near his pillow   was raised & he picked it
        & the correction became
        overcorrected   it grew
        into gerbil   squirrel   foxlet   it grew
        into wolf & the wolf   bled & grew
        into landmass with fiords
        deep & pleasing   it grew
        till one day   it became the UK
        there was Scotland
        pitched   smeared
        & 25 years passed
        & he did go to London
        & it was indeed a rodent's haunch
        & he missed dark blue & silence   he wished
        he could tear at London till it became the sort of problem
that could be repainted   easily
by his mother
or his father
in a sort of
lavender

Salute

I did make some efforts
Sally came by
in the backyard
playing at drill sergeant
blowing imaginary whistles (not meanly)
laughing   measuring the all
between it all
& later
a silvery night
way out beyond the back fence where
the cows had cut up the sexless earth –
was I
translucent as axolotls
twirling in rushes, going hah! & mmm
to mud . . .
                . . . I do make some efforts
        flooded bedroom
     boundless doubt
leafless trees filled with sleeping things, hundreds
& hanging below them, more
But isn't everything so unusual! I mean   useful
The cows are singing
& Sally stands under the porchlight laughing
What? she laughs What?
then I left

The Embryo, Repeated

I know that I look the same / but I have manifested a lion
ripe & pumping giddily

I know that I look the same / but I have manifested a lion
present & unasked & ready

I know that I look the same / but I have manifested a lion
precise as mathematics

I know that I look the same / but I have manifested a lion
shoulders up against the wind

I know that I look the same / but I have manifested a lion
peace be upon the lion

I know that I look the same / but I have manifested a lion
& everyone always says how glamorous

I know that I look the same / but I have manifested a lion
as a prize

I know that I look the same / but I have manifested a lion
& how is this manifestation distinguished from all the other animals?

I know that I look the same / but I have manifested a lion
I said how is this lion distinguished from all the other animals?

I know that I look the same / but I have manifested a lion
a toll, a shimmer, a serious cloud, valuable, brief

I know that I look the same / but I have manifested a lion
behold, my lion

I know that I look the same / but I have manifested a lion
l'chayim l'chayim

I know that I look the same / but I have manifested a lion
it is beloved

I know that I look the same / but I have manifested a lion
in the kitchen

I know that I look the same / but I have manifested a lion
ah thunder!

I know that I look the same / but I have manifested a lion
& the urge for daylight is real

I know that I look the same / but I have manifested a lion
& a stag rutting in a meadow

I know that I look the same / but I have manifested a lion
a rare nocturnal lion

I know that I look the same / but I have manifested a lion
ta for noting how this lion is distinguished from the other animals

I have popped it into a segmented tray
I have left it to set at optimal temp

*

& bloody etcetera!
gawd

I owe Cath a letter
she wrote in April & now

it's almost September
I should phone Pam too

phone Pam write to Cath
tell them I'm moving

to latch back onto the hopeless dresses of
Sde Boker with my goy ex, or

to Whanganui, maybe
What is the time?

Notes

'Dedications' borrows dedications and final lines from books found in a BnB.

'The Embryo Repeats' (5): 'pbu' is shorthand for 'peace be upon'.

The 'Allemande' poems use the lettered notes of the western octatonic scale in the order found in Bach's Cello Suites.

'12:55 to Masterton': '//' is a sound effect to be read as 'd-din'.

'Sage Advice' is a found poem, using emails with my mum about the Talmud.

'Word' was inspired by an exchange with a customer at a bookshop.

'Different Sides of the Man' is a response to Patrick Pound's exhibition 'On Reflection', City Gallery Wellington, 2018.

'Wage Advice' is a mash-up of RNZ interviews with Mary Holm and a complete list of Israeli prime ministers.

The asterisked * text on p. 60 is from RNZ's reportage following the 2016 Kaikōura earthquake.

Epigraphs

Dorian Corey: *Paris Is Burning* (1990), dir. Jennie Livingston.

Ken Bolton: 'Double Trouble', *A Whistled Bit of Bop* (Vagabond Press, 2010), 9.

Charlie Darwin: A deliberate misquotation. The actual quote, by Charles Darwin, is: 'The sight of a feather in a peacock's tail, whenever I gaze at it, makes me sick!' Letter to Asa Gray, 3 April 1860, *Darwin Correspondence Project*, University of Cambridge.

Bernadette Bassenger: Played by Terence Stamp in *The Adventures of Priscilla, Queen of the Desert* (1994), dir. Stephan Elliott.

Karen Kamensek: Joshua Barone, 'Body Wax and Karate Chops: How to Stage a Philip Glass Opera', *NY Times*, 7 Nov. 2019.

Sophie Zawistowski: Played by Meryl Streep in *Sophie's Choice* (1982), dir. Alan J. Pakula.

Dr Ruth-Anne Tibbets: *The First Bad Man* by Miranda July (Scribner, 2015), 92.